DR. NIGAM'S LABORATORY
NEW DELHI
3:05 P.M
WHY BOTHER? WE ARE ALL LIFE.
JUST BECAUSE THERE IS A SLIGHT DIFFERENCE IN SIZE ...
I NAMED MY PROTOTYPE ANTIGEN BATCHES FOR THE PARVOVIRIDAE VIRUS EXPERIMENTS AFTER OUR PRESIDENTS, IN ORDER OF RULE.
BLOK BLOK
AGGRESSIVE LITTLE BASTARDS, THE PARVOVIRIDAE.
GULP
THEY TOOK DOWN PRASADS AND RADHAKRISHNANS AND HUSAINS AND ON AND ON TILL THE NINTH PRESIDENT BATCH, THE SHARMAS.
S D SHARMA SWORE IN THREE PRIME MINISTERS DURING HIS TERM.

MY SHARMA BATCH MIGHT SUCCESSFULLY ERADICATE THE EXISTENCE OF THE P-STRAIN.
NOT THAT I WOULD DO THAT.
IT'S INTERESTING TO KNOW THAT THE SHARMA BATCH HAS THAT POWER THOUGH.
THANK GOD FOR THE NINTH PRESIDENT!
BRRR
THAT IS MY WIFE CALLING. NO, THAT IS NOT HER REAL NAME. YES, VETALA LIKE VIKRAM AND VETALA.
Incoming -
VETALA
SHE IS THE VETALA TO MY VIKRAM. SEE, VETALA MADE VIKRAM BETTER.
BEFORE WE GET OUT OF HERE FOR THE DAY, A COUPLE OF REMINDERS TO SELF. REMINDER #1 ...
BUT VETALA ALSO WAS ONE ANNOYING LEECH OF AN IMP SOMETIMES.

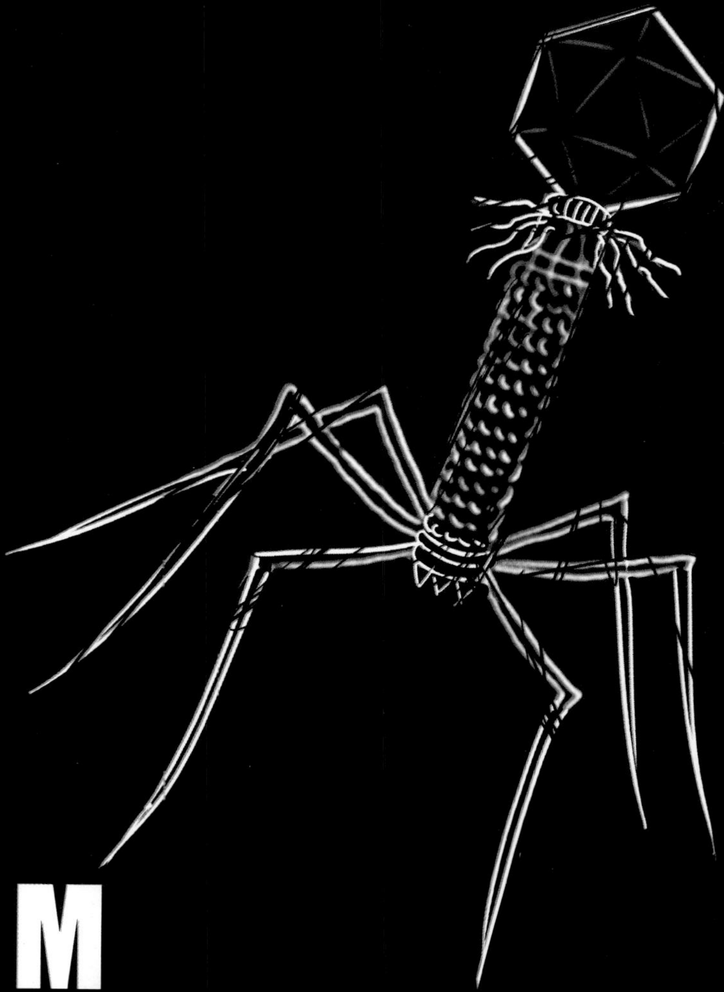

# DOCTOR M

## CREDITS:~

| | |
|---|---|
| Concept and Visualisation | Dr.Harsh Nigam/Karan vir Arora/ Shashank Avvaru |
| Chief Editor/Creative Director | Karan Vir Arora |
| Script | Shashank Avvaru |
| Pencils | Revin |
| Colorist | Bhakt Ranjan |
| Cover | Revin/Bhakt Ranjan |
| Letters | Rohit Rojal |

Doc M Subtitled Antham Published by
Kalapani Comics a division of Vimanika Comics

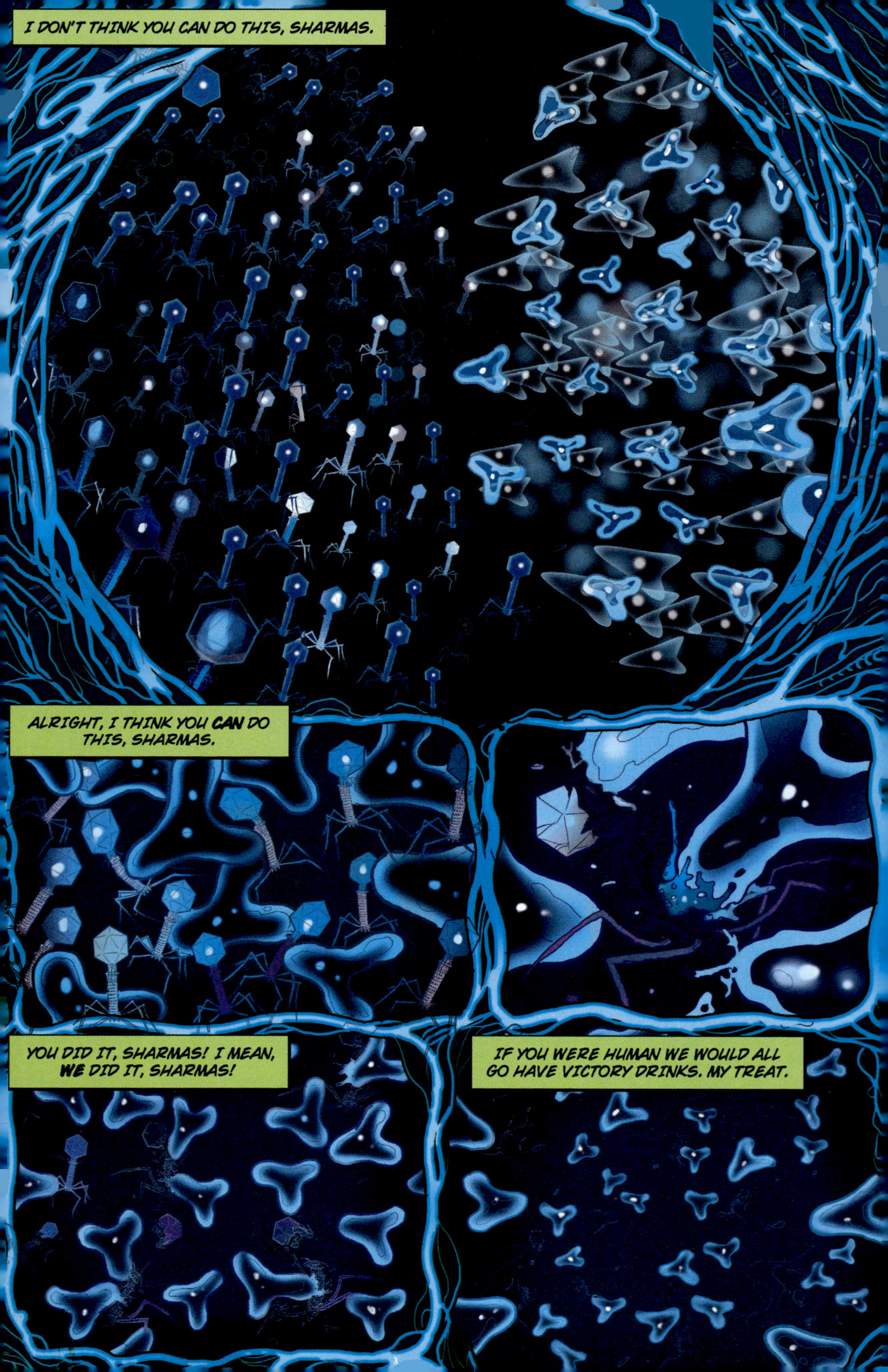
I DON'T THINK YOU CAN DO THIS, SHARMAS.
ALRIGHT, I THINK YOU **CAN** DO THIS, SHARMAS.
YOU DID IT, SHARMAS! I MEAN, **WE** DID IT, SHARMAS!
IF YOU WERE HUMAN WE WOULD ALL GO HAVE VICTORY DRINKS. MY TREAT.

CLEAN THE SINK TOMORROW.
BEFORE WE **BREED** A NEW DISEASE, INSTEAD OF PREVENTING THEM LIKE WE ARE SUPPOSED TO.
THIS NEEDED CLEANING YESTERDAY. OR A MONTH AGO.
... THE PRIME MINISTER HOPES FOR A FUTURE OF PEACEFUL CO-EXISTENCE WITH PAKISTAN.
-THE STOCK MARKET CLOSED WITH A SLIGHT HIGH TODAY-
-SCIENCE NEWS: RESEARCH GROUP FROM OSMANIA UNIVERSITY CLAIMS TO HAVE GOTTEN ONE STEP CLOSER TO SOLVING THE AIDS EPIDEMIC-
< VETALA
COME HOME ASAP. IT IS TINKU. IT IS VERY, VERY BAD.
-AT A LECTURE TO PROMOTE HIS NEW BOOK "HOW TO SURVIVE AN ALIEN INVASION", DR. SUNDARI SAID-

-THE BEST THING TO DO IS HIDE; FIND AN UNDERGROUND TUNNEL, ALWAYS HAVE A WEAPON; SPICES ARE SURPRISINGLY-
COME HOME ASAP. IT IS TINKU. IT IS VERY, VERY BAD.
WHAT ABOUT TINKU? WHAT IS IT?
-OR IF YOU PLAN TO FIGHT FIND THE CLOSEST ARMY HEADQUARTERS-
IT IS VERY, VERY BAD.
WHAT ABOUT TINKU ? WHAT IS IT ?
TINKU IS DYING.
-AND WITH THAT CONTROVERSIAL RELEASE, OUR SCIENCE NEWS BROADCAST CONCLUDES.
TINKU IS DYING.
AND NO DOCTOR KNOWS WHY.
IN LOCAL NEWS, A SUSPICIOUS VEHICLE HAS BEEN REPORTED TO BE LOITERING IN THE VICINITY OF VARIOUS PRIMARY AND MIDDLE SCHOOLS IN NEW DELHI TODAY.
NO CHILDREN HAVE BEEN REPORTED TO BE MISSING OR ASSAULTED.
THE VEHICLE IN QUESTION, A SILVER TATA INDIGO, WAS EARLIER REPORTED STOLEN IN CONNECTION WITH A HATE CRIME BY ANTHAM.
ANTHAM IS A RADICAL GROUP OF INDIVIDUALS CONTINUING TO WALK THE LINE BETWEEN NEO-TERRORISM AND TERRORISM.
THEIR ATTACKS HAVE BEEN THEATRICAL AND RELY HEAVILY ON SPREADING FEAR BUT THERE HAVE BEEN NO HUMAN CASUALTIES SO FAR.
JOIN US TOMORROW AT 3 FOR A SPECIAL ON ANTHAM AND TERRORISM WITH SPECIAL GUE-
FM 103

CLICK
WHEN ARE THEY GOING TO UNDERSTAND US?
THIS COVERAGE IS DRIVING ME CRAZY.
I WANT TO WALK IN THERE AND PULL THEIR TONGUES OUT.
YEAH ... ERR, ERR ... WHEN ARE THEY?
KERIWALA STREET
NEW DELHI
HAHAHAHA ...
I SO WANT TO TAKE A PHOTO OF YOUR FACE AND PASTE IT ALL OVER THE INTERNET.
YOU ARE PISSING YOUR PANTS, AREN'T YOU? THIS IS PEANUTS COMPARED TO SOME OF MY OPERATIONS IN BURMA.
AS I SHOULD BE! NIRMAL, YOU DON'T UNDERSTAND-
SLAAAP!
THIS IS YOUR LAST WARNING!
USE MY REAL NAME AGAIN AND I WILL WRING YOUR NECK!

WIPE YOUR GODDAMN FACE. I HAVE TOLD YOU A MILLION TIMES NOT TO USE REAL NAMES.
WE HAVE CODES FOR A **REASON**. EARS EVERYWHERE,
NEVER KNOW WHO MIGHT BE SNOOPING AROUND.
IF THE GOVERNMENT WANTS TO DO SOMETHING, THEY SHOULD SEND **EVERYONE** TO A FREE DRIVING SCHOOL FOR A YEAR BEFORE THEY PUT THEM ON THE ROAD.
WOULD SAVE US SO MUCH **TIME**.
BRIGHT HOPE SCHOOL OF EXCELLENCE
EDUCATION IS LIFE

PUT IT ON, AND STOP GRUMBLING.
... THEY, THEY ARE CHILDREN, R. LITTLE **CHILDREN**.
LIKE MY SISTER.
THEY WILL THANK US FOR IT ONE DAY. THEY WILL **CELEBRATE** US.
ANTHAM.
ANTHAM.

$*@#!
HOW DID THEY FIND OUT?!
IF THEY FOUND US THEY WOULD HAVE STOPPED NEXT TO OUR CAR, DUMBASS.
SCREEEEEECH!
PROBABLY A BOMB THREAT. PROBABLY JUST PRECAUTION.
OR MAYBE THEY FOUND OUT ABOUT US AND ARE THROWING US OFF BY NOT TARGETING US.
JUST MESSING WITH YOU, E. CALL OUR BOLLYWOOD FRIEND.
WE ARE GOING TO DO THIS OLD SCHOOL. I HOPE YOU WERE GOOD AT CARGO TRAINING.
CARGO?

SUMMER, THE YEAR BEFORE
... YOU HAVE TO STOP BREATHING DOWN THAT KID'S NECK. HE IS NINE YEARS OLD. DO YOU EVEN REMEMBER WHAT YOU DID WHEN YOU WERE NINE?
I REMEMBER FINDING MY ART TEACHER PRETTY. I WANTED TO KISS HER. I ALSO REMEMBER THINGS STARTING TO GROW DOWN THERE.
I DO NOT REMEMBER BEING AT THE BEACH AND READING A BOOK. RUN AROUND, EAT SOME SAND ... HECK, EVEN SWIM TO THE WATER! BUT A BOOK? ON A BEACH?
NINE WAS WHEN IT STARTED FOR ME TOO. PROBABLY TEN WHEN THE KICKS CAME.
BUDDY, TINKU IS NOT GOING INTO THE WATER BECAUSE HE KNOWS HE IS TOO SMALL TO DROWN. HE IS NOT GOING TO EAT SAND BECAUSE HE KNOWS IT IS UNHEALTHY.
YOU ARE QUESTIONING A KID'S CHOICES BECAUSE THEY ARE SMART.
NO, I AM QUESTIONING HIM CHOOSING PAPER OVER THIS VIEW.
SHUT UP. TINKU IS THE SMARTEST KID I KNOW. HE WILL BE JUST FINE.
TINKU! TINKU BETA, COME DOWN HERE!
EYY TINKU, SLOW DOWN! I AM NOT GOING TO SPEND MY WEEK IN GOA NURSING YOU BACK TO HEALTH.

.... RIGHT. UNCLE QUENTIN!
WHO IS THAT? UNCLE IS FINE, OR DOCTOR M IF HE WANTS TO MAKE ME SOUND COOL.
SCIENTIST FROM THE BOOK SERIES HE IS READING NOW. I ... I DON'T EVEN WANT TO START GOING THERE.
FAMOUS FIVE
FAMOUS FIVE! UNCLE QUENTIN!
FAMOUS WHO?
I AM STILL WORRIED.
WORRIED ABOUT WHAT?
TINKU.
... OH, TINKU.

NOW
OH, TINKU.
DO NOT GO IN THERE.
WHERE IS HE?
NIGAM, STOP PUSHING. CALM DOWN!
RESHMA, HELP US!
I AM A DOCTOR FOR GOD'S SAKE.

OH, TINKU.

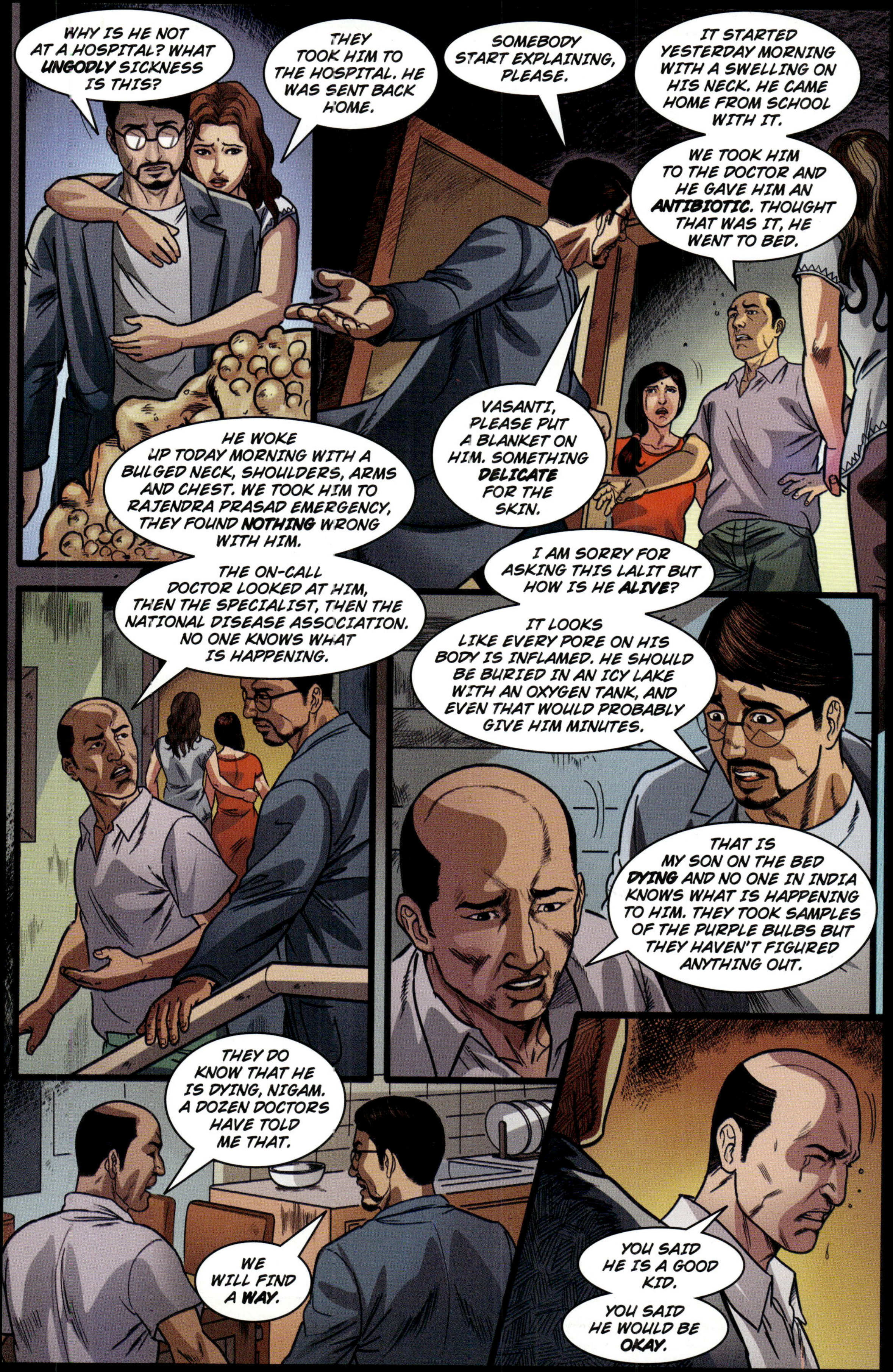
WHY IS HE NOT AT A HOSPITAL? WHAT UNGODLY SICKNESS IS THIS?
THEY TOOK HIM TO THE HOSPITAL. HE WAS SENT BACK HOME.
SOMEBODY START EXPLAINING, PLEASE.
IT STARTED YESTERDAY MORNING WITH A SWELLING ON HIS NECK. HE CAME HOME FROM SCHOOL WITH IT.
WE TOOK HIM TO THE DOCTOR AND HE GAVE HIM AN ANTIBIOTIC. THOUGHT THAT WAS IT, HE WENT TO BED.
HE WOKE UP TODAY MORNING WITH A BULGED NECK, SHOULDERS, ARMS AND CHEST. WE TOOK HIM TO RAJENDRA PRASAD EMERGENCY, THEY FOUND NOTHING WRONG WITH HIM.
VASANTI, PLEASE PUT A BLANKET ON HIM. SOMETHING DELICATE FOR THE SKIN.
THE ON-CALL DOCTOR LOOKED AT HIM, THEN THE SPECIALIST, THEN THE NATIONAL DISEASE ASSOCIATION. NO ONE KNOWS WHAT IS HAPPENING.
I AM SORRY FOR ASKING THIS LALIT BUT HOW IS HE ALIVE?
IT LOOKS LIKE EVERY PORE ON HIS BODY IS INFLAMED. HE SHOULD BE BURIED IN AN ICY LAKE WITH AN OXYGEN TANK, AND EVEN THAT WOULD PROBABLY GIVE HIM MINUTES.
THAT IS MY SON ON THE BED DYING AND NO ONE IN INDIA KNOWS WHAT IS HAPPENING TO HIM. THEY TOOK SAMPLES OF THE PURPLE BULBS BUT THEY HAVEN'T FIGURED ANYTHING OUT.
THEY DO KNOW THAT HE IS DYING, NIGAM. A DOZEN DOCTORS HAVE TOLD ME THAT.
WE WILL FIND A WAY.
YOU SAID HE IS A GOOD KID.
YOU SAID HE WOULD BE OKAY.

GO GET SOME SLEEP, SOMETHING TO EAT. I WILL BE HERE
EAT? WHILE MY SON IS DYING IN FRONT OF ME?
WHAT ARE YOU GOING TO DO? DIE OF STARVATION? YOU HAVE BEEN CRYING SO MUCH ALL YOUR ENERGY CAME OUT THROUGH YOUR EYELIDS.
I AM ALWAYS SO ANGRY AT HIM FOR WANTING TO READ BOOKS. WHAT KIND OF A SCREWED UP MOTHER AM I?
VASANTI, THIS IS NOT THE TIME FOR SELF CRITICISM. WE NEED TO MAKE SURE WE ARE DOING EVERYTHING IN OUR POWER TO CURE TINKU.
YOU THINK THERE IS A CHANCE?
THERE ARE SEVEN BILLION PEOPLE ON THIS PLANET.
SOMEONE SOMEWHERE MUST HAVE HAD THIS, SOMEONE MUST HAVE CURED IT AND SOMEONE MUST HAVE RECORDED THIS.
THE FACT THAT NO ONE HAS HEARD OF THIS MEANS IT IS PROBABLY CURABLE, JUST VERY VERY RARE. NOTHING IS MORE POPULAR IN THIS WORLD THAN AN UNCURED DISEASE.
I KNOW YOU WANT TO HELP HIM. I REALLY DO.
BUT, HONESTLY ...
... I WOULD RATHER LET HIM DIE THAN BE EXAMINED BY YOU.

BRIGHT HOPE SCHOOL OF EXCELLENCE
EDUCATION IS LIFE
AT THIS POINT IT IS JUST A PRECAUTION. IF WE NEED THE KIDS EVACUATED WE WILL CALL. WE DON'T KNOW WHAT THESE PEOPLE'S M.O IS YET.
THERE IS ALWAYS SOMEONE OUT THERE DOING THEIR BEST TO MAKE SURE YOU DON'T HAVE A GOOD DAY.
THAT IS WHY WE ARE HERE. GO BACK TO YOUR OFFICE. LET EVERYTHING CONTINUE AS NORMAL.
WHAT DO THESE PEOPLE WANT WITH INNOCENT LITTLE CHILDREN?
THERE IS NO RIGHT ANSWER TO SUCH QUESTIONS, MA'AM. THESE ARE TERRORISTS.
NEO-TERRORISTS.
TERRORISTS. THEIR MOTIVES START OFF WITH YOU BEING SCARED AND DOING SOMETHING IRRATIONAL.
RATHOR, THE VEHICLE IN QUESTION IS A TATA INDIGO, CORRECT?
YEAH, WHAT ABOUT IT?
WHAT IS IT, RAJI? YOU HAVE TO TALK TO ME.
THIS CANNOT BE LIKE RAJASTHAN. REMEMBER WHAT HAPPENED BECAUSE YOU GAVE ME THE SILENT TREATMENT?
WHUB
YOU GOT SHOT IN RAJASTHAN BECAUSE YOU DIDN'T MAKE OUT THE CONVICT TEN FEET BEHIND YOU.
JUST LIKE YOU DIDN'T NOTICE THIS!

GODDAMMIT!
DID YOU CALL HIM, E? YOU HAVE NO IDEA HOW MUCH MY GROIN HURTS RIGHT NOW.
YES I DID. HE WAS DRINKING IRANI CHAI. AGAIN.
THAT MORON AND HIS OBSESSION WITH IRANI CHAI ... PFFFT.
1.5 KM AWAY
JFC 2016 REVIVAL
IRANI CHAI
Fresh & Healthy
TOKO EMAS
Soedarj
BEST QUALITY GOLD
... THAT IS WHY THIS IS **OUR** DEAL.
COME ON, RAJ. YOU OWE ME 250 ALREADY. IT IS REALLY **HARD** TO BUY MILK AND CHAI PATTI NOW.
HOW ELSE WILL I GET YOU TO KEEP **TALKING** TO ME, CHOTU?
I AM CUTTING YOU OFF!
THE CHAI WAS GREAT, CHOTU.

CHUTHIYE!
SECURITY GUARD AT BAJRANG LAL PRIMARY SAID SOMETHING ABOUT A **GAS MASK**.
ANY ITEMS OF SUSPICION REPORTED APART FROM THE CAR?
LIKE THE WORLD WAR II GAS MASKS?
I GUESS SO. HE SAW SOMEONE AROUND THE CAR HOLDING IT AT SOME POINT.
GAS MASK MEANS CHEMICALS. CHEMICALS MEANS **BAD NEWS**. I DON'T LIKE THIS.
I'LL REQUEST **BACKUP** AND SWITCH ALL SCHOOLS TO A HIGH ALERT.
HEAR THAT?
**MOTORBIKE**. POSSIBLY CONVERTED. GET IN THE CAR AND DUCK.
PUTT!
PUTT!
PUTT!
PUTT!
ALWAYS FIGHTING UNFAIR, **MAA KA**!

THIS IS INSPECTOR RATHOR! PURSUING RIDER - JUST CROSSED BRIGHT HOPE - POSSIBLE SHOTS FIRED, FIRE RETURNED-
THOSE WEREN'T SHOTS, RATHOR.
THEY WERE FIREWORKS.
THAT'S GOOD, RIGHT?
IT IS A DISTRACTION. THEY WILL COME BACK FOR THE CAR. WE DON'T HAVE LONG.
WATCH AND LEARN.
FSSSSSS

I AM THE TURTLE WITH THE SWORD.
NO, I AM THE SWORD TURTLE.
YOU GOT TO BE HIM LAST TIME.
THAT WAS TRILOK!
DO YOU WANT US ALL TO GET PUNISHED? SHUT UP! PICK ANOTHER TURTLE.
LOOK! LOOK UP!
BUBBLES!

IS THIS WHAT THE PT PERIOD IS FOR YOU?!
WHO BROUGHT A BUBBLE MAKER TO SCHOOL?
HAND THEM OVER NOW OR NO AFTERNOON BREAK FOR THE ENTIRE CLASS.
OKAY THEN! NO BREAK FOR-
BUT TEACHER!
SHSHH!
WHAT IS IT, MUNI?
EXCUSE ME, TEACHER. THE BUBBLES CAME FROM THE TREE UP THERE. IT WAS NONE OF US!
IT'S TRUE, TEACHER. NO ONE BOUGHT BUBBLES.

LALIT! HOW COULD YOU SAY THAT? HE IS A DOCTOR! OUR CHILD IS DYING!
THE DISEASE ASSOCIATION HAS THEIR BEST PEOPLE LOOKING FOR A CURE. THESE ARE PEOPLE WHO HELPED FIND A CURE FOR EBOLA.
AND HE IS NOT A DOCTOR!
NEVERTHELESS-
YOU ARE NOT A DOCTOR! NOT A REAL ONE, ANYWAY.
YOU DON'T WORK IN A HOSPITAL. YOU DON'T DO SURGERY.
YOU MAKE YOUR OWN POTIONS LIKE A WITCH IN A CAVE. MOST OF THEM ARE PLACEBO, I AM SURE, AND THEY ONLY WORK BECAUSE I AM SURE YOUR HOMEOPATHIC MEDICINES CONTAIN ALL THE INGREDIENTS OF A REGULAR PILL.
YOU ARE A MODERN DAY WANNABE SUSHRUTHA WITH A PERSONAL AGENDA! IN THE TWENTY YEARS THAT WE HAVE BEEN NEIGHBORS, HAVE WE EVER COME TO YOU WITH A MEDICAL PROBLEM?
NO!
WE NEVER WILL EVEN IF MY SON LAYS DYING! GOD ONLY KNOWS HOW YOU LIVE WITH YOURSELF AND FEED TRISHA AND-
NOW, LALIT, SAY WHATEVER YOU WANT ABOUT ME ... THAT'S FAIR GAME.
BUT ONE WORD ABOUT MY FAMILY AND YOU WILL SEE THIS "WANNABE SUSHRUTHA" TURN INTO NARASIMHA HIMSELF AND TRUST ME, YOU WILL NEVER SPEAK AGAIN.
I WILL MAKE SURE OF IT.

VASANTI, DO YOU TRUST ME? IF THERE IS EVEN A SNOWBALL-IN-HELL CHANCE THAT WE MIGHT SAVE TINKU, DO YOU CONSENT TO ME TAKING IT?
... YES.
THEN VASANTI, PLEASE FORGIVE ME FOR THIS.
WHAT ARE YOU DOING?!
STOP!
LET ME GO! LET ME GO!
OW! MY BACK!
THUD!

HAPPY TO HAVE GOTTEN THAT OUT OF YOUR SYSTEM?
HUH?
CLICK!
CLICK!
LOCK THIS DOOR. BARRICADE IT. LADIES, ANYTHING YOU CAN DO TO KEEP HIM IN THERE ... DO IT.
BANG!
BANG!
I WILL BREAK THIS DOOR, DOC! I AM NOT KIDDING!
YOU ARE TOO CHEAP TO DO THAT, LALIT.
VASANTI? ARE YOU REALLY CHOOSING NIGAM OVER ME?!
I AM CHOOSING A DOCTOR OVER A BUSINESS MANAGER TO SOLVE A MEDICAL PROBLEM.

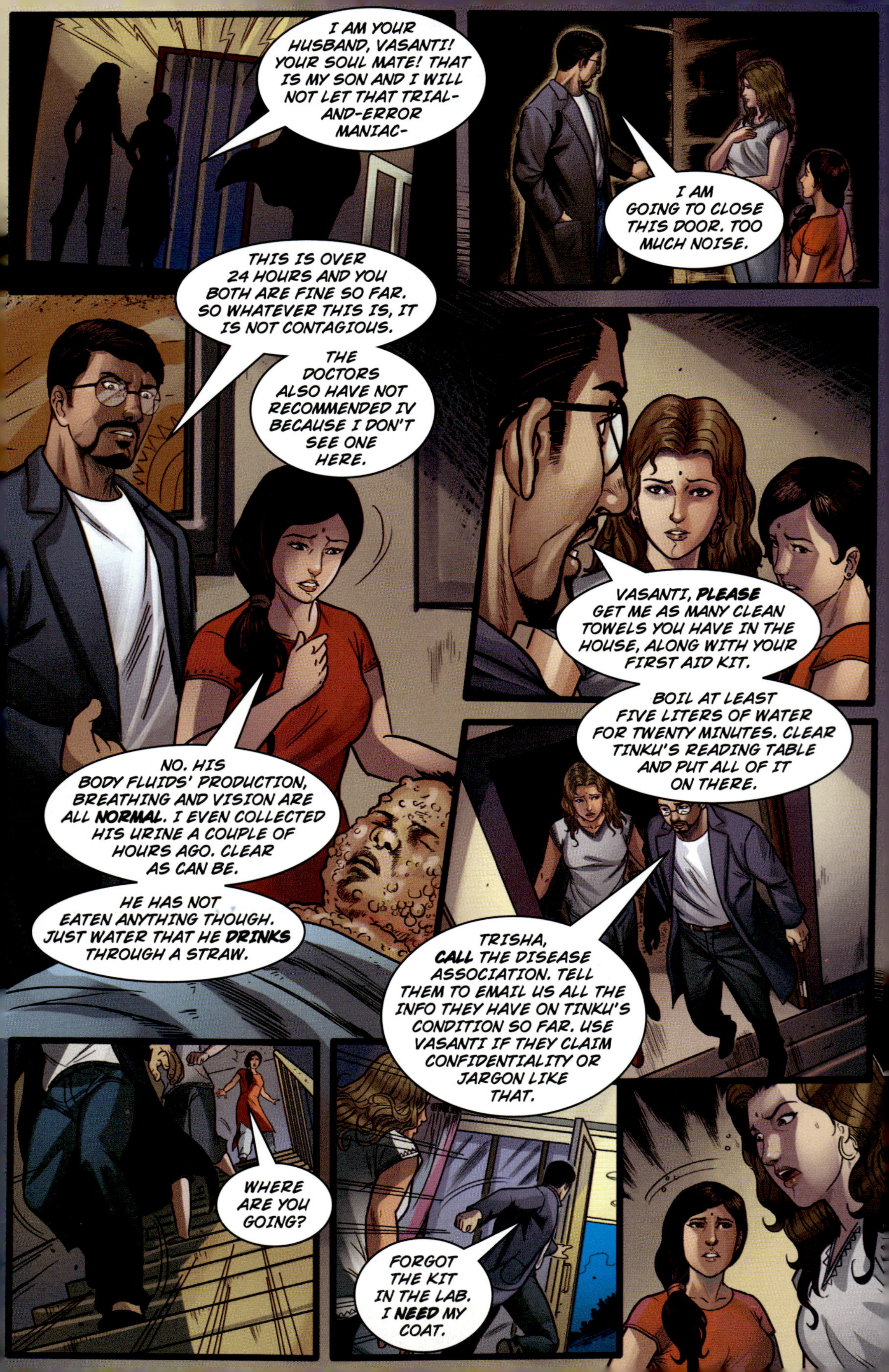
I AM YOUR HUSBAND, VASANTI! YOUR SOUL MATE! THAT IS MY SON AND I WILL NOT LET THAT TRIAL-AND-ERROR MANIAC-
I AM GOING TO CLOSE THIS DOOR. TOO MUCH NOISE.
THIS IS OVER 24 HOURS AND YOU BOTH ARE FINE SO FAR. SO WHATEVER THIS IS, IT IS NOT CONTAGIOUS.
THE DOCTORS ALSO HAVE NOT RECOMMENDED IV BECAUSE I DON'T SEE ONE HERE.
NO. HIS BODY FLUIDS' PRODUCTION, BREATHING AND VISION ARE ALL NORMAL. I EVEN COLLECTED HIS URINE A COUPLE OF HOURS AGO. CLEAR AS CAN BE.
HE HAS NOT EATEN ANYTHING THOUGH. JUST WATER THAT HE DRINKS THROUGH A STRAW.
VASANTI, PLEASE GET ME AS MANY CLEAN TOWELS YOU HAVE IN THE HOUSE, ALONG WITH YOUR FIRST AID KIT.
BOIL AT LEAST FIVE LITERS OF WATER FOR TWENTY MINUTES. CLEAR TINKU'S READING TABLE AND PUT ALL OF IT ON THERE.
TRISHA, CALL THE DISEASE ASSOCIATION. TELL THEM TO EMAIL US ALL THE INFO THEY HAVE ON TINKU'S CONDITION SO FAR. USE VASANTI IF THEY CLAIM CONFIDENTIALITY OR JARGON LIKE THAT.
WHERE ARE YOU GOING?
FORGOT THE KIT IN THE LAB. I NEED MY COAT.

WHAT IS THAT?
NO NO NO! NOT THE COAT! I HAVE SEEN THE COAT! YOU WILL NOT TOUCH MY SON WITH IT!
I AM BACK. VASANTI, EVERYTHING SET?
YES, EVERYTHING YOU HAVE ASKED FOR IS ON TINKU'S DESK. I AM BOILING ANOTHER 5 LITERS JUST TO HAVE A BACKUP.
YOU ARE A GOOD MOM, VASANTI.

BANG!
BANG!
DOC, I WILL KILL YOU IF YOU USE THAT MADNESS ON HIM. AT LEAST LET HIM DIE IN PEACE ... -SOB-
THAT KID ON THAT BED IS LIKE MY SON TOO. MY LIFE MEANS NOTHING IF I DON'T DO WHAT I BELIEVE I CAN TO SAVE HIM.
HOMEOPATHY MIGHT BE MUMBO JUMBO TO YOU BUT IT IS LIFE ITSELF TO ME.
IF TINKU IN THERE DIES AND I AM STILL ALIVE, YOU CAN SATIATE YOUR RAGE BY KILLING ME.
IS THAT A GOOD DEAL?
.... SAVE MY SON. PLEASE. -SOB- -SOB-
OKAY, TINKU ...

... I HOPE YOU ARE READY FOR THIS.
ORGANON

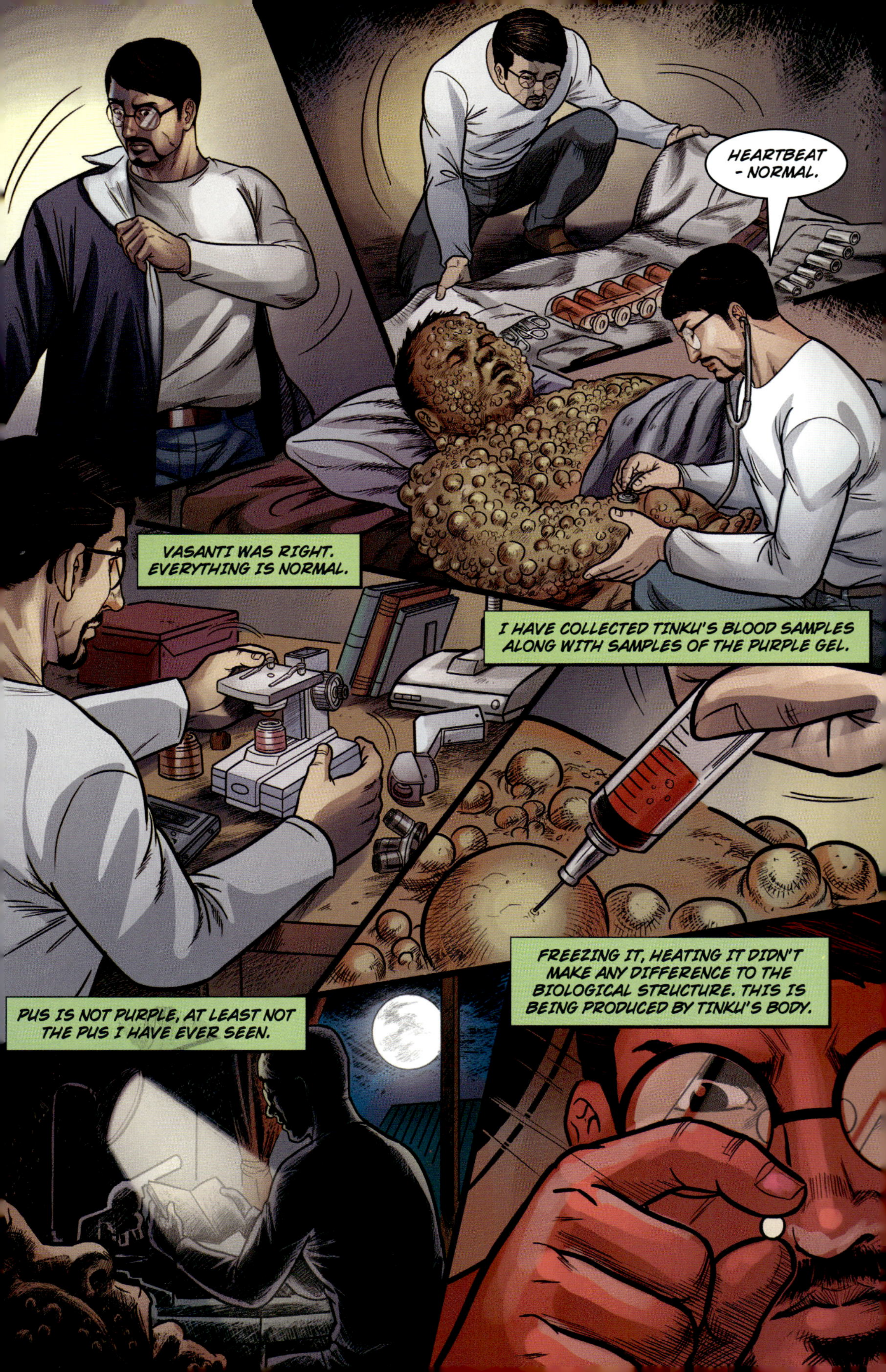
HEARTBEAT - NORMAL.
VASANTI WAS RIGHT. EVERYTHING IS NORMAL.
I HAVE COLLECTED TINKU'S BLOOD SAMPLES ALONG WITH SAMPLES OF THE PURPLE GEL.
PUS IS NOT PURPLE, AT LEAST NOT THE PUS I HAVE EVER SEEN.
FREEZING IT, HEATING IT DIDN'T MAKE ANY DIFFERENCE TO THE BIOLOGICAL STRUCTURE. THIS IS BEING PRODUCED BY TINKU'S BODY.

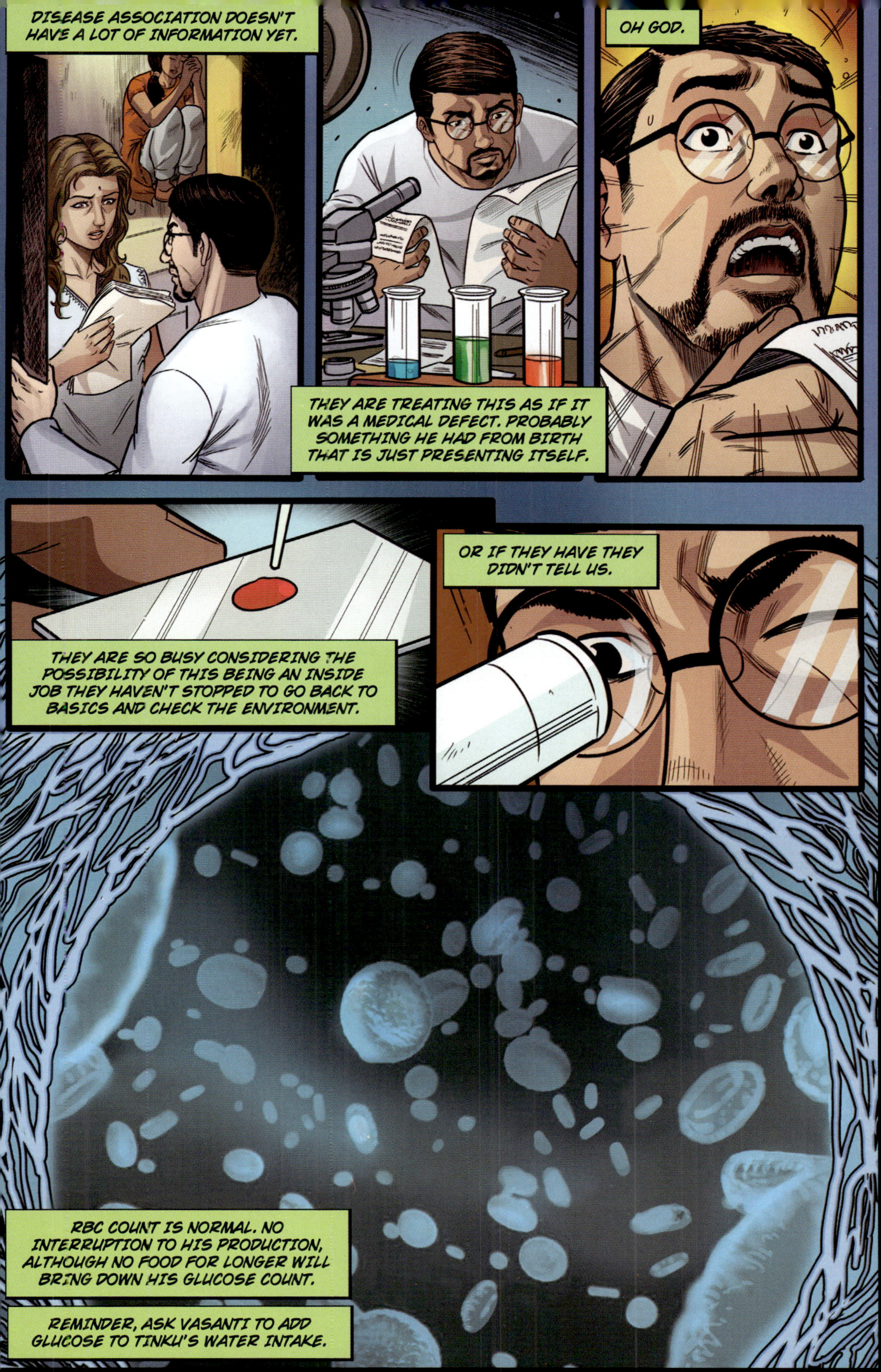
DISEASE ASSOCIATION DOESN'T HAVE A LOT OF INFORMATION YET.
THEY ARE TREATING THIS AS IF IT WAS A MEDICAL DEFECT. PROBABLY SOMETHING HE HAD FROM BIRTH THAT IS JUST PRESENTING ITSELF.
OH GOD.
THEY ARE SO BUSY CONSIDERING THE POSSIBILITY OF THIS BEING AN INSIDE JOB THEY HAVEN'T STOPPED TO GO BACK TO BASICS AND CHECK THE ENVIRONMENT.
OR IF THEY HAVE THEY DIDN'T TELL US.
RBC COUNT IS NORMAL. NO INTERRUPTION TO HIS PRODUCTION, ALTHOUGH NO FOOD FOR LONGER WILL BRING DOWN HIS GLUCOSE COUNT.
REMINDER, ASK VASANTI TO ADD GLUCOSE TO TINKU'S WATER INTAKE.

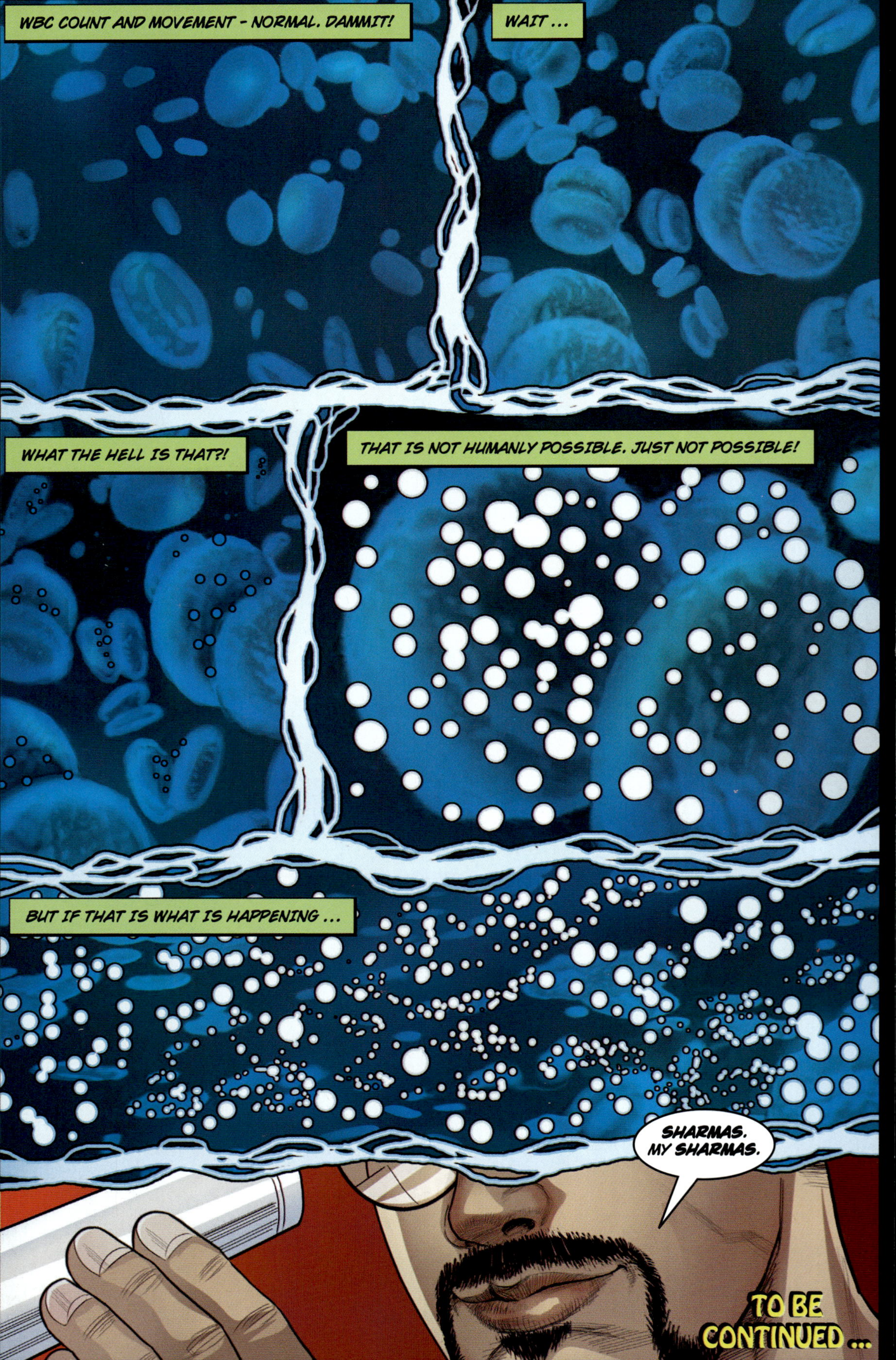
WBC COUNT AND MOVEMENT - NORMAL. DAMMIT!
WAIT ...
WHAT THE HELL IS THAT?!
THAT IS NOT HUMANLY POSSIBLE. JUST NOT POSSIBLE!
BUT IF THAT IS WHAT IS HAPPENING ...
SHARMAS. MY SHARMAS.
TO BE CONTINUED ...

# Concept Art Explorations

by Revin

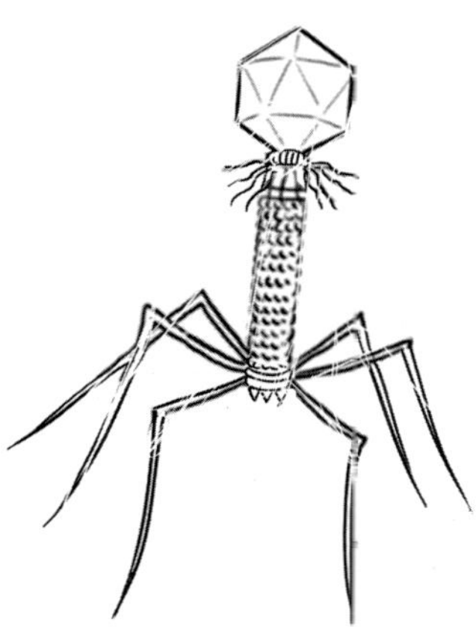

DOC MAVERICK

KaGED
MUSCLE
Kalapani
Vol 1
First ever fitness based
action graphic noval
PAIN
ORDER NOW!!!